101 REASONS
Hillary Will
Make a Great
President!

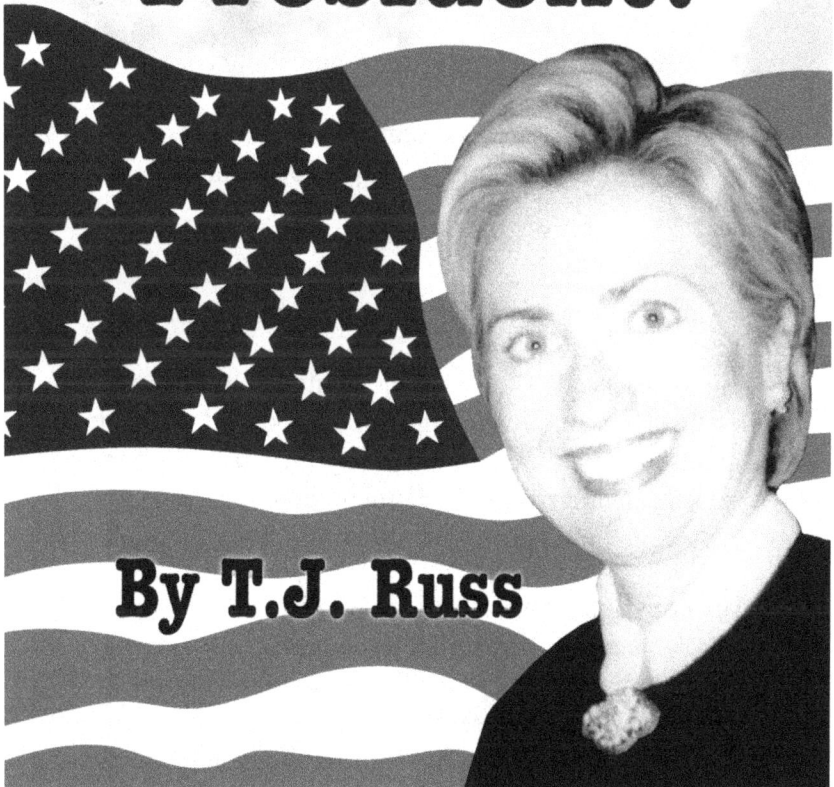

By T.J. Russ

OTHER TITLES BY T.J. RUSS:

Everything President Obama is Doing to
Keep America Free, Strong, and Prosperous

The Audacity of Hype

The Obama Border Agency

Obama 2012: The Case for Re-Electing Barack Obama!

- -

Terence Storm Publishing

Web: www.TerenceStormPublishing.com

This publication is designed as a parody and
is meant for humorous purposes only.

ISBN: 1-933356-71-5

INTRODUCTION:

Are You Offended by This Book?

We hope not! This book is intended to make you laugh... not get angry. It is a novelty product that utilizes the old fashioned comedy of parody. This is a style of comedy that goes back to the 16th century. The Random House Dictionary of the English Language says "Parody" is "a humorous or satirical imitation of a serious piece of literature or writing."

Parody has been used throughout history as a fun way to make social and political points. In today's world of dirty politics where people say and do all kinds of very negative and offensive things, we feel that this form of comedy is more appropriate.

So don't get angry that this book is blank. Have a good laugh. This is the intention of this book and hopefully the person who provided this book to you. We kept the price low, so even those who purchased it not realizing it was a parody book would not be upset.

Besides being a fun political statement, the blank pages inside this book can be used as a journal, sketch pad, address/phone book, diary, or any number of other ideas. Be creative!

But we do hope this book upsets some people who might be thinking about voting for Hillary. After all, Donald Trump doesn't call her "CROOKED HILLARY" for no reason! This book gives you all the reasons why Hillary deserves to be President. Buy a copy for all the Hillary lovers in your life.

Finally, if you love this book and want to order large quantities, visit www.TerenceStormPublishing.com.

REASON #1

REASON #2

REASON #3

REASON #4

REASON #5

REASON #6

REASON #7

REASON #8

REASON #9

REASON #10

REASON #11

REASON #12

REASON #14

REASON #15

REASON #16

REASON #17

REASON #18

REASON #19

REASON #20

REASON #21

REASON #22

REASON #23

REASON #24

REASON #25

REASON #26

REASON #27

REASON #28

REASON #29

REASON #30

REASON #31

REASON #32

REASON #33

REASON #34

REASON #35

REASON #36

REASON #37

REASON #38

REASON #39

REASON #40

REASON #41

REASON #42

REASON #43

REASON #44

REASON #45

REASON #46

REASON #48

REASON #49

REASON #50

REASON #51

REASON #52

REASON #53

REASON #54

REASON #55

REASON #56

REASON #57

REASON #59

REASON #60

REASON #62

REASON #63

REASON #64

REASON #65

REASON #66

REASON #67

REASON #68

REASON #69

REASON #70

REASON #71

REASON #72

REASON #73

REASON #75

REASON #76

REASON #77

REASON #78

REASON #79

REASON #81

REASON #82

REASON #83

REASON #84

REASON #85

REASON #87

REASON #88

REASON #89

REASON #90

REASON #91

REASON #93

REASON #94

REASON #95

REASON #96

REASON #97

REASON #99

REASON #100

REASON #101